THE
BARBER'S
DILEMMA

AND OTHER STORIES FROM
MANMARU STREET

Koki Oguma

Text in English: Gita Wolf

The Artist and his Cat

My name is Koki Oguma, and I'm an artist.
I live on Manmaru Street with my cat, Kuro.
There are always lots of people coming
and going in my neighbourhood, and I
like that. Some days I like to sit and watch
people as they go about their day, and at
other times I stroll around Manmaru Street,
with no particular plan. Lots of ideas
come to me, so I go home and start to
doodle. Sometimes I'm not sure what I'm
scribbling, so I start talking to my doodle,
to find out more. And then I find myself
thinking: 'Hmm...that's a good story...'

Kuro's footprints

flowers from footprints

The Barber's Dilemma

Mr. Kenji is our barber. Sometimes he is not sure of himself. One day a man with a terrific moustache came to the barber shop, and Mr. Kenji was in a dilemma.

One moment he was timid, thinking:

"How am I going to cut all this hair? What if my scissors break?"

The next minute he grew bold and thought: "What an opportunity! I'm going to give this man the finest moustache in the world!"

Take a Seat

When Ms. Isuyo is tired, she's grateful when she finds a chair.

One day she was struck by a thought:

"Don't chairs need a rest too?"

So she went looking for all the chairs she could find, and gently put them on herself.

Soon a lot of tired little creatures came around to rest on the chairs. But Ms. Isuyo doesn't notice them at all.

The Stream

A small stream runs behind our street.
And there you can find Mr. Isoda, fishing.

Once while he was sitting by the stream,
he heard the sound of water flowing, and
began to wonder:

"Does the river speak a language? Can I
learn it?"

He listened carefully, and practised the
sounds day after day. At first it didn't go
well, but he kept trying, until he sounded
exactly like the stream. One day a shoal
of fish entered his mouth, thinking that
they were swimming upstream. Mr. Isoda
didn't mind at all.

Ms. Kiyoko

When she's in the juice bar on Manmaru Street, Ms. Kiyoko drinks orange juice. It usually sounds like this:

"blub... blub... blub..."

When Mr. Pupu sits behind her, he leans forward to listen. He likes the sound, and finds it comforting.

Magic Pockets

On Syoko's birthday, her mother sewed
her a colourful jacket. The best thing
about that jacket were the pockets. When
Syoko opened them, one by one, she
found very strange things inside.

Close the pockets quickly, Syoko, before
the snakes and crocodiles get into a fight!

The House of Stairs

Ms. Danko loves to climb. She's built herself a house of stairs that looks just like her in every way. The stairs are never ending: they go on and on, higher and higher. Ms. Danko is happy all day, she never needs to come down.

The Friendly Seaweed

In the noodle bar on Manmaru Street, Mr. Siota ordered a soup. To his surprise, the seaweed in the soup rose up, and putting a friendly arm around his shoulder, began chattering away like they were old friends:

"How do you like the soup?"

"Better if you drink it slowly!"

"Any particular girl you like?"

"What's your plan for the day?"

"I just want to eat in peace!" thought Mr Siota. "Now, what's the best way to eat this seaweed?"

The Cream Hat

My neighbour Ms. Kurata loves cream.
She likes it so much that she makes
cream hats for herself. One day I told
her how much I admired her hats—what
beautiful shapes and textures they had.
So she made me a surprise gift of a cream
hat, and I put it on to go out. It was great
to start with, but then the cream began to
run down my head and my face became
all sticky.

So I said to Ms. Kurata, "This hat melts!"

"That's the best thing about cream hats!"
Ms. Kurata exclaimed.

Hmm...I'm not so sure.

Sweet Tooth

There is a sweet shop on our street, and Mr. Mituru is their best customer. He has a really sweet tooth. Sadly, he doesn't brush his teeth too well either — so all in all, he has really bad teeth. One day his teeth got so bad that they popped out of his mouth, and began dancing around.

"Ha, ha, look at me! I'm the worst tooth in the world!"

"Can't catch me!"

"Want this dance?"

"Music! We need music!"

They were having a great time. Mr. Mituru looked at them, and popped a sweet into his mouth.

"Maybe time to go the dentist..." he thought.

The Cactus

Ms. Matsuoka loves her cactus. She loves it so much that she wants to hug it.

"Ouch! These spines hurt!" she shouts.

Mr. Matsuoka overhears her, and comes over to help. He removes the worst spines, one by one.

"Thank you!" says Ms. Matsuoka.

"You're welcome." says Mr. Matsuoka. "Come and give me a hug, I don't have any spines!"

Sweet and Sharp

Mr. Sato likes two things: he likes
sweets, and he likes to sing. His singing,
unfortunately, is not sweet. It's hoarse
but sharp, like fiery red pepper. One day
he decided to combine his two loves and
made himself a guitar out of candy. Pretty
soon lots of little animals came around,
and began to lick the guitar. When he
started singing though, they all ran away.

Mr. Tuchida's House

Mr. Tuchida wanted to build a house on his head. He called the builders, and they started piling bricks on his head. Things went well, and it looked as though a great big house was coming up. The only thing was that the whole thing got a bit heavy, and Mr. Tuchida's neck began to bend under the weight. One of the builders gently put a cold compress on Mr. Tuchida's neck. He was a very kind man.

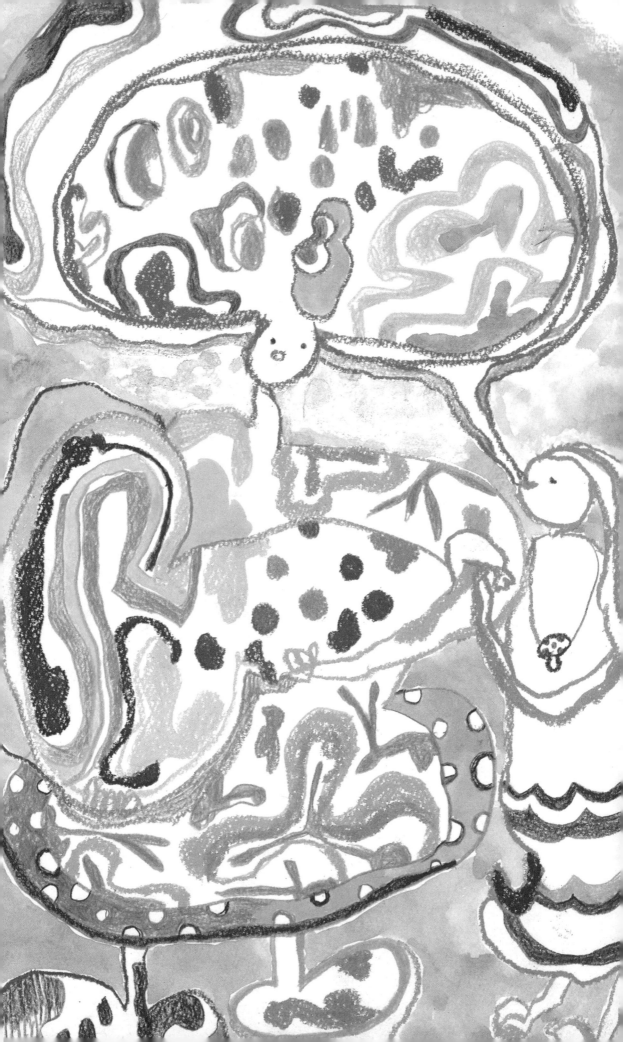

Mushroom

Mr. Kiyota's girlfriend likes mushrooms. So one day he showed up in a great big mushroom costume: mushroom clothes, mushroom hat, mushroom shoes.

In his hand was a special present for her: an enormous mushroom. It was really wonderful!

So what does Mr. Kiyota's girlfriend like better? The mushroom? Or Mr. Kiyota?

He's not sure.

The Boots

Here's Mr. Yosuke, stamping along the street. He's got on his favourite super long boots, and he's having a great time. It's just rained.

Splash! Splash! Mr. Yosuke splatters water as he walks along happily. He's a mild man, usually, but today he doesn't care who he splashes with muddy water. He's having too much fun. That's the thing about the rain, the boots and Mr. Yosuke: it's a great combination.

The Shadow

When people are sad, they cast a long shadow behind them. Mr. Naganuma was walking along Manmaru Street one day when he saw a woman trailing a very long shadow.

"Oh dear!" thought Mr. Naganuma. "What can the matter be?"

He got closer, and began munching away at the shadow.

"Wonder what it tastes like..." thought Mr. Naganuma. "Will I get sad too? Will this lady feel better?"

The Candy Slide

Ms. Oda likes sweets, so she made a giant candy. It turned out a bit funny, like a huge slide. So she set it up on the playground and invited her friend Ms. Ono to try it out.

"Whee!" shouted Ms. Ono as she slid down, licking the candy as she went...

"That's pretty good!" thought Ms. Oda. "If they ever have a Slide-Down-the-Candy-As-You-Lick-It competition, I can enter Ms. Ono as a contestant. I'll be the coach."

The Necklace

Ms. Momo's son makes her a very special present. It's a necklace made of mud and stones. It's a bit large and squashy, but Ms. Momo loves it. She puts it on over her favourite pink dress and the dress gets muddy and sticky. Ms. Momo doesn't mind at all.

"It's beautiful!" she says to her grinning son.

The Cheese Cap

Mr. Hiroshi and his children like cheese.
So he's made himself a cap of cheese.
His son and daughter have brought
candles close to the cheese cap and
they're all eating the melting cheese
with great relish.

It's getting a bit warm for Mr. Hiroshi
though, but he hasn't said anything yet,
since he doesn't want to spoil the fun for
the kids. But he's going to protest, pretty
soon.

The Traffic Light

A strange thing happened the other day on our street. The traffic signal suddenly began to dance! Red, orange, green...the lights began to twinkle away, in any order they liked.

Surprised cars ran into each other, and people started yelling.

"Hey!"

"Stop messing around!"

"My car's wrecked!"

"I'm going to be late!"

Some people didn't find it so bad — they even liked it.

"That's a cool dance!"

"Ha, ha, happy lights!"

Lots of different feelings that day, on Manmaru Street.

Kuro

Hmm...there does seem to be a lot happening in my neighbourhood. I can hardly keep up with painting. But my faithful cat Kuro is always ready to help. Here he is, nibbling at a painting, wondering what it tastes like. Careful Kuro, don't chew up the artist!

The Barber's Dilemma and Other Stories from Manmaru Street

Copyright © 2017 Tara Books Private Limited

For the illustrations: Koki Oguma

For the text: Koki Oguma and Gita Wolf

Design: Catriona Maciver

For this edition:
Tara Publishing Ltd., UK
www.tarabooks.com/uk
and Tara Books Private Limited, India
www.tarabooks.com

Production: C. Arumugam

Printed in India by Canara Traders and Printers

ISBN: 978-93-83145-65-2